American Girl

by Julie Murray

Abdo Kids Jumbo is an Imprint of Abdo Kids
abdobooks.com

abdobooks.com

Published by Abdo Kids, a division of ABDO, P.O. Box 398166, Minneapolis, Minnesota 55439.

Abdo Kids Jumbo™ is a trademark and logo of Abdo Kids.

Printed in the United States of America, North Mankato, Minnesota.

102025

012026

Photo Credits: Alamy, Getty Images, Shutterstock, ©Joetography LLC p.7/CC BY-SA 2.0, ©Seth Poppel/Yearbook Library p.7, ©The Strong National Museum of Play, Rochester, New York, p.9, ©grilled cheese p.13/CC BY-ND 2.0

Production Contributors: Teddy Borth, Jennie Forsberg, Grace Hansen
Design Contributors: Candice Keimig, Pakou Moua

Library of Congress Control Number: 2025936510

Publisher's Cataloging-in-Publication Data

Names: Murray, Julie, author.

Title: American Girl / by Julie Murray

Description: Minneapolis, Minnesota : Abdo Kids, 2026 | Series: Toy mania! | Includes online resources and index.

Identifiers: ISBN 9798384907565 (lib. bdg.) | ISBN 9798384908265 (ebook) | ISBN 9798384908616 (read-to-me ebook)

Subjects: LCSH: American Girl dolls--Juvenile literature. | Dolls--Juvenile literature. | Character dolls--United States--Juvenile literature. | American girl's series--Juvenile literature. | Toys--Juvenile literature. | Toys--History--Juvenile literature.

Classification: DDC 688.7221--dc23

Table of Contents

American Girl

American Girl dolls combine play, imagination, and learning. From historical to **custom**-made dolls, American Girl has been loved since 1986!

americangirl.com/service
American Girl
American Girl
As seen in World By Us
Maritza Ochoa
8+
smart girl's guide
American Girl
MAKING A DIFFERENCE
using your talents and passions to change the world
Carly Cushnie for American Girl

Inspiration Strikes!

Pleasant Rowland was a teacher and writer. She took a trip to **Colonial** Williamsburg in Virginia. She loved how history was brought to life there. She wanted her students to be interested in learning too.

Pleasant Rowland
JAMES CRAIG
JEWELLER
Engraving
Watch-Making
Done in the beft manner

Rowland later went doll shopping with her nieces. There were very few dolls to choose from. **Inspiration** struck! She could make dolls and storybooks that taught people about history.

Addy
Walker
Luciana
Vega
MEET
ADDY
An American Girl
1864
Book 1
NASA

Each book would be about a young girl during a time in history. Rowland wanted to make the dolls and their stories **accurate**. She had **experts** research clothes and other details that were true to certain times and places.

Rebecca Rubin
Kaya
Samantha Parkington
Rebecca
1914
RUBIN
Kaya
176

Rowland started the Pleasant Company in 1986. It first sold the dolls and their storybooks through **catalogs**. People purchased the dolls using a mail order form.

Happy New Year, Julie Book $6.95
new! Paperback
PA-92919
In her third book, Julie spends time with Ivy's family as they prepare for the Chinese New Year.
Julie's Pet Bunny $20
new! Julie's bunny, Nutmeg, comes with a basket bed and carrots.
PA-F6312
Ask your mom if this popular '70s toy made her wish list when she was a girl!
Julie's Christmas Gift $18
new! In her day, Julie may have asked for a Barbie® styling head with a set of six curlers (three shown) and a brush.
PA-F6324
Julie & Ivy celebrate change
Ivy's Chinese New Year traditions inspire Julie to greet the New Year with a fresh outlook
Julie's Christmas Outfit $24
new! When she goes to the fancy Fairmont Hotel for tea with Dad and her sister, Tracy, Julie wears this crushed velvet jumper over a puffy-sleeved, lace-trimmed blouse. Includes gold metallic tights and shiny sandals.
PA-F6571
Ivy's New Year Outfit
PA-F7130

The Pleasant Company's first dolls were Samantha, Kirsten, and Molly. Each doll came with clothes, **accessories**, and books. They were a hit!

Kirsten
Larson
Samantha
Parkington
Molly
McIntire
Addy
Walker

Getting Dolled Up

Rowland sold her company to Mattel in 1998. The same year, American Girl Place opened in Chicago, Illinois. The store sells dolls, clothes, and **accessories**. It also has a restaurant, hospital, and hair salon!

Guided by Rowland's vision, Mattel has released many new dolls and collections. Girl of the Year features a new doll and story each year. Create Your Own allows kids to make dolls and clothing that reflect them!

Create your own
CREATE
A DOLL THAT MATCHES YOUR STYLE AND SPIRIT!
DESIGN
ONE OF A KIND APPAREL.

Over the years, many more stores have opened around the world. There have even been movies and plays based on American Girl. Rowland's vision of bringing learning to life lives on!

ACADEMY AWARD® NOMINEE ABIGAIL BRESLIN IS
KIT KITTREDGE
An American Girl
American Girl
McKenna
SHOOTS FOR THE STARS
American Girl
Isabelle
Dances Into The Spotlight
SPACE CAMP
SCIENCE GLOVEBOX

More Facts

- There are more than 100 different American Girl dolls. Over 36 million dolls have been sold!
- There are fun **accessories** for the dolls. Vehicles, pets, and furniture are just a few.
- American Girl dolls were **inducted** into the National Toy Hall of Fame in 2021.

Glossary

accessories – items added on to something to make it prettier or more complete.

accurate – free of mistakes or error.

catalog – a printed or digital publication that lists and displays products available for purchase.

colonial – related to the thirteen colonies that became the United States.

custom – made specially for a particular person.

expert – someone who knows a lot about a particular thing.

inducted – brought in as a member.

inspiration – an idea or creative spark.

Index